Respect Yourself

Becoming the Woman God Made You to Be

Calvin M. Hooper

Contents

Introduction

Chapter One..............................Receive the Revelation

Chapter Two...............................Retrieve Your Identity

Chapter Three........................Remain Focused on the
King's Perspective of You

Chapter Four....................Realize Your Story Has Value

Chapter Five.............Refuse to Compromise Who You Are

Chapter Six................Resolve to Have Godly Boundaries

Chapter Seven..................Recognize God's Man for You

Chapter Eight...Final Words

Copyright © 2015 Calvin M. Hooper and Living Faith Publications.
All Rights Reserved.
Unless otherwise noted, all scripture references are from the NASB and NKJV version

Introduction

What is respect? The word defined means *esteem for or a sense of the worth or excellence of a person, a personal quality or ability, or something considered as a manifestation of a personal quality or ability.* Respect is something that all women long for. The unfortunate thing is that so many women look for respect from others without first respecting themselves.

We all frequently compare ourselves favorably with someone else. We all think or have thought of someone we consider less mature, less competent, or less able than we are. That person is a great comfort to us because he or she enables us to keep our self image intact by saying, "Well, at least I'm not like so and so." The only problem with determining our self worth by comparing ourselves with others is that we are using the wrong measuring stick. A little boy came up to his mother one day and said to her, "Mommy, guess what! I'm eight feet, four inches tall!" His mother, greatly surprised, inquired into the matter and found he was using a six-inch ruler to measure a foot. "The boy was actually only a few inches taller than four feet. That is exactly what we do; we measure ourselves by one another, an imperfect prototype, rather than by the standard of the word of God. One author once said: *It seems to me that many women can't seem to get a grip on the power that they possess, and forever see themselves as being in a position whereby they have to compete and prove their worth - rather than being in a position where they already understand their worth... Dr. Dennis Neder*

So many women fail to acknowledge their worth and respect themselves. Too many women are looking for acceptance, love and respect without first understanding that you have to accept, love and respect yourself before you can get the type of acceptance, love and respect you need and deserve. What is it that causes women to fail to see their worth, and fail to see themselves the way God intends for them to? I read a story once about self respect in regards to women that I believe explains what happens. The story said:

I believe self-respect is very important to everyone, especially vital for women. It should be the first important quality we should have rather than anything else.

When you fail to respect yourself, many behaviors will be like giveaways. The way you talk to yourself and others is an announcement of how you feel about yourself. The way you allow others to talk about you and treat you is another giveaway. Another giveaway is when you believe you don't deserve to be heard or to be spoken to with dignity, which reveals that your self-respect is low. Of course you don't hear yourself say " I don't deserve happiness". But listen to others around you, how do they talk to you, and how do you talk to them. You hear yourself starting statements by saying "I know you don't want to hear this, but...." or "I am not sure about this, you decide...." You demean your message even before you say a word!

Your family, friends, and others will treat you the way you teach them to treat you. If you expect respect and give it in return, that sets up an atmosphere for everything you want. If you are self-disrespecting, that is what others will give you. So when you are not treated with respect, you should do something about it. If someone treats you disrespectfully, you should treat them politely and at the same time explain that you will not stay around for their abusive behavior. So stop self- disrespecting, and doubting yourself, throw these negative thoughts away. Think of what you want, what you expect, and set an example yourself. You will then definitely get respect from others. Law of attraction never fails.

YOU ARE THE ONE RESPONSIBLE TO CHANGE OTHERS' VIEW OF YOU. (End quote) Maybe you are reading this and you're saying, "Pastor Hooper, yes, that is me. I need to change how I think of myself and change how others see me. I want that, but how do I get there?"

This book is something God inspired me to write to help you get and maintain HIS perspective of you. I pray that this book helps you to become the woman God has made you to be.

Chapter One

Receive the Revelation

Psalm 139:14 says... *I will give thanks to You, for I am fearfully and wonderfully made;*

This book is based on that verse. There is much more that is said in that Psalm 139, but I believe the path to attaining and maintaining God's perspective of you begins here.

Let's examine two words in this verse. The first is **fearfully**. What does that mean? In the original Hebrew language, the word used for fear was *yare*, and its meaning depended on the context of what was being said. In some contexts, it relates to terror and fright. In other contexts, it means **honor, respect and awe**. Of course in the context of this verse it is easy to see that it means honor, respect and awe. The second word, **wonderfully,** in the original language is the word *pala*, which means **to be wonderful, be marvelous, and be amazing**. It also means **to show a wonder or cause to astound**. It is God's word that gives this revelation. The revelation comes from God. Since it is His word that reveals that you are **fearfully and wonderfully made,** you should not doubt it but accept it. Here's an exercise for you. Point at yourself and say **I AM FEARFULLY AND WONDERFULLY MADE!** Consider yourself special in God's eyes. In His eyes you are **honored, respected and an awe inspiring woman. You are wonderful, marvelous, amazing. You are a wonder and astounding!** Receive the revelation! It is what you are! For many of you and women you know, when you look in the mirror what you see is anything but fearfully and wonderfully made. You hear what God's word says, but the image you see won't allow you to receive it. You know you should respect the person you see looking back at you in the mirror, but you have no *esteem for or a sense of the worth or excellence of that person.* Why does this happen?

Here is why I believe this happens...

1. **You try to gain a sense of self worth from those around you rather than from God.** No offense to any woman reading this, but as a woman you tend to be much more emotional than a man. Therefore, you can be a much harder critic of yourself and you seek validation, acceptance, and a sense of self worth

from what others say instead of what God says. If you are seeking this validation, acceptance and sense of self worth from people who don't have a godly sense of self worth, but rather have a worldly sense of self worth, OR who don't have a relationship with God at all, then you are already heading down the wrong path. Let me take a moment and explain what I mean by a worldly sense of self worth. The real you is the spiritual part of you. The external part of you can and WILL change! Too many women focus on developing the external portion, but their spiritual part is still in need of attention. That's why so many Christian women look like the world, act like the world, and have the same values as the world. Things that they think they HAVE TO do to the external parts are really things that they have been told by the world that they have to do. For example, some will spend money on weave, nails, eyelashes, surgeries and more to dress up the externals when they really do not HAVE TO. Remember, you are fearfully and wonderfully made. As I heard somebody say before, "God don't make no junk!" Let me say that you are NOT in sin if you use these enhancements, but in many cases it's not that these are used that is the problem, but the problem is that they are often overused and many times not needed at all.

2. **You have allowed yourself to start repeating what others have said about you.** The Bible says in Proverbs 23:7 (KJV)... *For as he thinketh in his heart, so is he...* The problem for many women is that they are not operating according to what THEY think, but according to what OTHERS think. As a result, women feel like they are unworthy to strive for great accomplishments. Stop letting others shackle your destiny and get in tune with God's plan and purpose for you. What can you imagine yourself doing? You have the power in your hands to bring about a life of prosperity. Let me give you some scripture references that highlight this point. Joshua 1:8...*This book of the law shall <u>not depart from your mouth</u>, but you shall <u>meditate on it day and night</u>, so that you may <u>be careful to do according to all that is</u>*

<u>*written in it;*</u> *for then you will* <u>*make your way prosperous, and then you will have success*</u>. I underlined some key portions of that verse for your benefit. If God has given you the formula for success, it does not matter what others have said. Start saying what God has said about YOU! Psalms 1:1-3...*How blessed is the man who does not walk in the counsel of the wicked, nor stand in the path of sinners, nor sit in the seat of scoffers! But his delight is in the law of the* LORD, *and in His law he meditates day and night. He will be like a tree firmly planted by streams of water, which yields its fruit in its season and its leaf does not wither; and in whatever he does, he prospers.*

3. **You are stuck in the past due to a traumatic event.** Sexual abuse, physical abuse, verbal abuse, rape, abandonment, are some of the things you may have been through and it may seem like as much as you try to smile your way through each day, month and year, you still feel like that traumatic event is just as fresh in your mind as the day it happened. Maybe it seems like you're just about over it, and then

something happens to trigger bad memories. You try to establish relationships with men to move on with your life, but because of past experience, you either connect with someone just like the one that abused you, or you chase away the one that God has really sent, and who can do you some good. I preached a series of messages on Relationships, Love and Sex, and one part dealt with Rape and Sexual abuse using the story found in 2 Samuel 13:1-20. If you struggle with this trauma, there is a helpful document I found and have referenced in my teaching before that can be found and downloaded here:

http://www.shbi.org/content/BibleLessons/studysheets/Abuse.htm

Of course, this is not an exhaustive list of reasons women have no self worth, but I believe they are some of the big ones. God has a plan for everyone's life and we are all full of purpose and destiny. Once you can receive the revelation then it's time to retrieve your identity.

Chapter Two
Retrieve Your Identity

To retrieve simply means *to bring back to a former and better state; restore.* Many of you may be scarred by years of dishonor, and disrespect. You haven't felt wonderful in years. In fact, the only wonder you've had is wondering how you got so emotionally wrecked. You haven't felt marvelous; you've felt marvel less. The only amazement you've had is the amazement that you are still trying to find your identity after all this time. You may feel like you've made too many mistakes or you've got too much to fix or too many layers of pain, hurt, and disappointment to peel off to retrieve who you really are. I know that some of you may be reading this looking for strength to continue to cope with your emotional despair until you can get to the next book, conference, retreat or whatever else. Some of you may be looking for a band aid to patch up your hurt and take your eyes off the damage that's been done. For some of you, you've been carrying baggage around for years that have continually kept you looking back and defining yourself by your mess ups, mistakes, blunders, bad relationships, and misguided advice. I want to ask you the question Jesus asked the man at the pool of Bethesda, "Will you be made whole?" When he was asked the question, the man did what many of us do, rather than giving a direct answer, he began complaining about why he was still in the condition he was in. You would think that after 38 years the man would instantly respond with an emphatic YES I DO! Rather than responding to the words of the Lord in such a positive manner, the man started making excuses! With his response, you'd have to wonder if perhaps the man was sick in his head. He started considering that it had already been so long. His excuses were justification, in his opinion, to why he was still ill. He said I don't have anyone to put me in the pool (nothing more than blaming others for why it has been so long). He then said, while I am coming, someone steps down before me. (In other words, I try to do it, but someone always gets in my way). The man was in a pitiful condition, and his condition caused him to be stuck right there waiting and hoping in something that was not even guaranteed to bring any degree of change. He was not willing to look any further than the pool for his change to come. He was making excuses with the Lord right there with him!

Many times the same question is presented to us in relation to the ills that affect us. Do you want to get well? Do you want to get better? Do you want to see your situation change? Do you want to be delivered? After all the things that some of us have been through, we ought to shout YES LORD, HEAL ME! But instead, we make excuses for why we still have bad habits; and we get stuck right there. We make excuses for why we are still ill from past hurt, and we get stuck right there. We make excuses for why we still struggle with feelings of guilt, and we get stuck right there. We make excuses for why we're still hindered from some moral failure and we get stuck right there. We make excuses for why we still allow ourselves to have low self esteem because of what somebody said about us, and we get stuck right there. We get stuck, and we don't move forward from that place. We stay there a long time, and it keeps us from being able to do anything else because we are so consumed with the problem. We know what the Word says but we keep putting our faith in things other than the Word of God.

We blame others to appease our conscience and try to justify our struggle. We keep making excuses, but the Lord is right there with us ready to set us free!

The text only gives us these excuses the man gave, but you can imagine that he probably continued to talk. Right then, Jesus, having heard enough, uttered the most profound words the man had heard in 38 years. I can only imagine that he probably heard a lot of stuff in 38 years. He probably heard things such as…Yeah; there he is, going to that pool again. I remember what happened to him. I remember how he got in such bad shape. He's been no good since. He's never going get over what he did. I don't even know why he thinks he can get better? I already told him he's wasting his time.

But now this man heard the words that would blow his mind. Jesus said, "Get up, pick up your pallet and walk!" When the man heard this, faith must have stirred in him. Romans 10:17 says,

So then faith cometh by hearing, and hearing by the word of God[1]

When he heard this, he took his mind off his excuses, he took his eyes off of what could not help him, and he looked to Jesus, the author and finisher of our faith, and in essence responded to the word of God since Jesus was God in the flesh! Change happened for the man! It wasn't the next day, it wasn't the next week, it wasn't the next month but he had a right now experience!

Jesus said a lot in those eight words...

1. When He said get up, He was essentially saying that He was tired of the man's excuses, tired of his pitiful state, and He was ready for the man's faith to come alive.
2. When He said pick up your pallet, He was making him mark the official end of 38 years of suffering, and he could look at that pallet and remind himself of

---

[1]*The Holy Bible : King James Version.* 1995 (Ro 10:17). Oak Harbor, WA: Logos Research Systems, Inc.

where he had been, and from where the Lord had brought him from.
3. And then Jesus said, Walk! He was to move forward, and get away from that place of infirmity where he had been stuck for 38 years.

In other words, Jesus was saying to the man and he's saying to you today, your excuses are weak, stop depending on others who can't help you to deliver you from your condition. Stop blaming others for why you've been so long in your condition.

Jesus is calling you to get up! You've allowed yourself to be stuck where you are too long! The Lord is saying hear my word; exercise your faith, GET UP, TAKE UP YOUR PALLET, AND WALK! Just like the man, God is not looking to bring about your change tomorrow, next week or next month, but He's looking to give you a right now experience.

Get up from bad habits now! Get up from past hurt now! Get up from feelings of guilt now! Get up from moral failure now! Get up from low self esteem now! Get up from an abusive childhood now! Get up from the pain of a failed marriage now! Get up from people who said you'd never be anything now! Get up from pride now! Get up from addictions now! Get up from Johnny don't love me and he said I'll never find another like him! GET UP!!! Take up your pallet, mark the end of that thing, remind yourself of what the Lord has done for you, and walk! Don't find your way back to that place, don't go back to the thing that kept you from moving forward, don't go back to what kept you in bondage and discouraged. Don't go back but keep walking, keep living holy, keep having faith in God, keep seeking His righteousness, and keep going up in the Lord. I'm talking to the people who aren't afraid to exercise their faith. Believe in the word of God and be changed right now! God wants to give you a right now experience!

Here was this man in the presence of the One who was literally, grace, and in the presence of the One who made the sacrifice to come to where He was, and all he could do was give excuses. What he thought he needed (getting in the pool) really wasn't what he needed at all. Here was Christ, God manifested in the flesh, right in front of this man, with the power to bring forth healing. I want to let you know, that God is with you right now as you're reading this and NOW is the time God wants to heal you! This is not a "strength to cope" book! This is not a band aid distribution moment, this is not a time to check and make sure you still have that useless baggage intact! It's not a time to complain and continue dwelling in misery! No, this is a time for deliverance, a time for healing, a time to retrieve your identity and respect yourself! This man had been dealing with this problem for a long time. His problem became a way of life for him. He lost hope, and he made excuses, but it wasn't until he responded to the word of the Lord that he was changed.

Not only is a right now experience needed to move forward in life, but God wants to use each of us, but we have allowed our situations to cause us to make excuses that hinder our usefulness for God. In response to those who make excuses why they cannot serve the Lord, Rick Warren writes:

Abraham was old, Jacob was insecure, Leah was unattractive, Joseph was abused, Moses stuttered, Gideon was poor, Samson was codependent, Rahab was immoral, David had an affair and all kinds of family problems, Elijah was suicidal, Jeremiah was depressed, Jonah was reluctant, Naomi was a widow, John the Baptist was eccentric to say the least, Peter was impulsive and hot-tempered, Martha worried a lot, the Samaritan woman had several failed marriages, Zacchaeus was unpopular, Thomas had doubts, Paul had poor health, and Timothy was timid. That is quite a variety of misfits, but God used each of them in his service. He will use you too if you stop making excuses.

God wants to change some of you right now, and all it takes is to stop making excuses, respond to His word, exercise your faith, get up, and watch Him make a difference in your life. You may be saying to yourself, yes I see and I accept who I am, but I've been to conferences, retreats, women's small groups, etc, in the past and thought I was fine, but after a few days I was feeling unworthy again "What do I do now? You must CHANGE your perspective of YOU!

Chapter Three
Remain focused on the King's Perspective

In the book of 2 Samuel there is the story of a man named Mephibosheth. Mephibosheth was the son of David's best friend, Jonathan, and the grandson of King Saul. When Jonathan and Saul were killed, Mephibosheth was about 5 year's old living under the care of his nurse. When she heard the news that Jonathan and Saul had been slain, she took Mephibosheth in her arms and began to flee. However, in her haste, he fell, and he became lame. Later in his life, King David, who had made a promise to Jonathan that he would not cut off his loving-kindness from his house forever, sought to fulfill that promise, and was told about the existence of Mephibosheth.

It's not hard to imagine that Mephibosheth probably experienced ridicule from others as a child due to his condition. Words that had been spoken to him in his early years probably resonated in his mind even as an adult. Before we came to Christ, we were spiritually lame, unable to please God, and satisfied with the lives we lived. We were ***dead in trespasses and sins...*** and we... ***walked according to the course of this world.*** However, life has happened and some of you are feeling spiritually lame and unable to please God even after you have come to Christ. Harmful words spoken to you continue to resonate in your mind, keeping you bound. Not only has that happened, but the devil, continued to show up in various ways to ridicule you about the past. Even as I speak to you through the pages of this book, some of you are plagued by memories of your past.

Mephibosheth lived in Lo-debar, which means "no pasture." When you think of a place with pasture you think of a place that's thriving and where growth can happen, but a place of no pasture is dead and it's a place of stunted growth. Before Christ, we all, in essence, lived in Lo-Debar. We had no pasture; there was no true satisfaction for our souls.

Mephibosheth was totally unaware of the change that was about to take place in his life. It was: Sudden, Unexpected, Totally undeserved. I believe that some of you will receive what God is saying and will experience a sudden, unexpected, totally undeserved change!

He was not seeking change. He was like we were before we were saved. We were lost, and by nature we did not seek God. But even after Mephibosheth was given unmerited favor, even after he was given an inheritance, even after he was adopted into the king's family, and even though he went from the place of no pasture, to having a seat at the kings table, Mephibosheth said," ***What is your servant, that you should regard a dead dog like me?"***

In other words, what have I done to deserve this?

He still felt unworthy! His question echoes the same sentiments many of you feel today! Many of you still feel unworthy! In the case of Mephibosheth, he didn't bring it on himself. He was just an innocent child who had an unfortunate thing happen. Now he's full grown and having to deal with the damage of the past. His story is a graphic depiction of how many of you may feel inside. Something happened that caused you to stumble, leaving you feeling like life has dropped you and you've felt lame and unworthy ever since. You may not have even brought it on yourself.

Some of you women have been living in Lo-Debar long enough. You've felt empty long enough. Your growth has been stunted long enough. The King is calling you to have a seat at His table. He's calling you to take your rightful place where you belong. The King has made promises to you and He is waiting for you to present yourself so He can fulfill His promises to you.

Mephibosheth lived in fear, but he did not know that he had no reason to fear because of the promise that had been made. He became content living in obscurity and accepted that as normal. He could not see what a blessing it was to be invited to the palace by the king. He probably thought about not going not only because of fear, but because he felt unworthy to receive such treatment. It's only speculation, but perhaps he had been made aware of the promise David made to his father Jonathan, but he decided he would play it safe and stay in Lo-Debar. He didn't want to reveal himself to the King because he felt he would receive judgment, which is what the King had a right to give because he was a descendant of the former King. He could have just been feeling him out when he asked *what is your servant, that*

you should regard a dead dog like me to see if this was the real deal or if this was some kind of trap! That is just like the emotional state of many women. They have become so accustomed to living in obscurity because of what has happened in their past. They grow to accept it as normal. In their case, they know God has made promises to them. They know God has a plan and purpose for their life. They've heard it all before. They've seen it in God's word. But they are afraid to reveal themselves to the King. They are afraid to open up their heart and let Him in, because in doing so they will be forced to confront the pain in order to let it go. Some are in this state because of bad seeds that have been planted in them. Maybe their mother told them they were no good. Maybe their father abused them verbally or physically and made them feel unattractive. For some, the absence of a father caused them to be victims of players running tired lines on them to get them to believe they love them so much and that they are what they need. When so many men approach them with the same game, they start believing all men are that way so there's no need in expecting anything else. Maybe their spouse has belittled, betrayed and berated them so much that they accept it rather than demanding respect. Many women are so emotionally wrecked that when the King calls they can't imagine being worthy of receiving the blessing of His promises. They can't receive the revelation that they are fearfully and wonderfully made. They can't receive the blessing that they are a daughter of the King and special in His sight. They can't receive the blessing of that man that God sends their way that knows God and sees them as God sees them. They can't receive that man who sees them as a person, not an object; someone with intellect, and intelligence, feelings and worth. They have become so used to the devil's men seeing them as someone with an attractive physique, pretty face, nice hair and other external attributes, that when someone looks beyond just the external attributes and shows interest in them as a person they can't digest what God's man is bringing to the table. They think something is wrong with him! They think he's got a hidden agenda and they are waiting to find out what's the catch. Does this sound like anyone you know? Does this sound like you? It's hard for them to see that there is no hidden agenda! It's simply the man God has sent to find you!

You need to stop looking at yourselves in the mirror, and telling yourselves what you are unworthy of. Stop reminding yourself of your past, and start walking in the liberty wherewith Christ has made us free, and be not entangled again with the yoke of bondage (Galatians 5:1). Whatever you need God to take from you in order for you to respect yourself and see yourself as God sees you, take it to God in prayer now. Present yourself before the King. He's calling you now. He wants to bless you now! Maybe you are that woman who was sexually abused, raped, and/or beaten. Maybe you were verbally abused, neglected, disrespected, and dishonored. Maybe you have been hurt by gossip or slander, and you have not been able to move forward. Maybe you have low self esteem or perhaps your self esteem is so low it's practically nonexistent. Maybe you were pressured into promiscuity or maybe you decided to go that route yourself. Lo-Debar is not your place of destiny! There is a better place. You are a child of the King. Jesus is here to heal every one of your hurts. You don't have to see yourself through the filter of the past anymore. You are fearfully and wonderfully made. It's not what you need to work to become, it's who you **already are**. God has so much in store for you. You have been hindered long enough. Now is the beginning of a new you!

It's time to receive the revelation that you are fearfully and wonderfully made. God's word said it and since it says it then you are all that! In fact, you are all that and more. Testify to yourself and say, I am more than the lies you told about me, I am more than the abuse I've suffered, I am more than the gossip my haters tell, I am more than what Ray Ray, Johnny, Pookie, Jimmy Mack, and all the rest of the players said about me! I am more than what the devil has been saying about me all these years! I am all that God says I am! I am fearfully and wonderfully made! Some of you purchased this book not really knowing what to expect, but one thing you did know was that you didn't respect yourself the way you should. You didn't feel like you were that special. I believe that as you hear yourself say to yourself that you are all that God says you are that a transformation is taking place. As you read this, you are seeing yourself from His perspective. You are fearfully and wonderfully made and now your soul knows that very well. Now that you have the King's perspective you need to move forward from where you are and don't look back! For many of you that may be easier said than done, especially since you may have lost a proper perspective of yourself years ago. I believe the next chapter will encourage all of you regardless of how long it has been to press forward and never again let yourself be hindered.

Chapter Four
Realize Your Story Has Value

God took special care in creating a woman. When he created man he took dirt, shaped it molded it, breathed into it and man became a living soul. Even though man was made from the dirt, he was still God's highest creation on Earth. God created mankind male and female. When God saw fit to make woman, God caused a deep sleep to fall upon Adam, and He took Adam's rib and formed Eve, and made her attractive to the man, and made her a help meet unto him. So woman is a delicate creature, yet also very strong. Notice that the woman was made from the rib of the man. The rib is designed to protect the delicate internal organs of the human body, but the ribs are themselves covered by muscle, fatty tissue, tendons and skin. So when God took the uncovered rib, now formed into a woman, she still needed a covering. So Adam was to cover her by caring for her, protecting her, loving her, nurturing her, and that's the treatment God still expects men to provide for their wives today. That's why Genesis 2:23-24 says…

And Adam said, this is now bone of my bones, and flesh of my flesh: she shall be called Woman, because she was taken out of Man. Therefore, shall a man leave his father and his mother, and shall cleave unto his wife: and they shall be one flesh.

Women have tremendous value. But sometimes, rather than being cared for, protected, loved and nurtured, the woman, who is delicate, yet strong by nature, encounters pain sometimes for years from a number of sources such as men who neglect or abuse her, family that has told her she will never be anything, female friends that turn their back on her and talk about her while they walk away from her. These things and more cause other issues that add to the pain such as low self esteem, depression, anxiety and other health issues, loss of motivation to pursue your dreams, and the list goes on. All of this causes her to be an emotional wreck. Women are strong, but they can break. Just like a rib, even broken or fractured, she can still function. So many women have things in their past that have broken them, but through the years they've managed to function, and have managed to smile and mask the fact that they are broken. I believe that AS YOU READ THIS, a release from your brokenness is present now!!! Many women struggle for years and on the outside they look fine, but on the inside they're messed up, broken, and hurting. Many women share in the testimony of the woman with the issue of blood. You may not have the same issue she had, but you are hemorrhaging. You're hemorrhaging low self esteem, depression, and painful memories. You're hemorrhaging from vicious words such as: you're too skinny, too fat, too short, too tall, your hair isn't long enough, your lips are too big, you don't have lips at all, etc. You may be hemorrhaging from the pain of a divorce, loveless marriage, moral failure, or failure to accomplish a long time goal or dream. Maybe you're still struggling with the fact that a sperm donor made a baby with you but didn't want to have a life with you. Maybe you feel used and abused because you're always taken for granted. The list can go on and on, but the point is that you've got something or some things in your life that are a constant problem for you. You know you want to get past it, get over it, get beyond it, put it totally in the past and move on, but you feel trapped, stuck and without an answer on how things can get better. It seems like your situation is never going to change and you keep getting worse year after year. You've got a smiling face, but smashed emotions. On the outside you look like you've got it all together, but on the inside you've got some issues. You're broken, but still functioning. You do well to give the appearance of moving forward in life, after all, you don't want to walk around all day every day talking about your issues and throwing your own perpetual pity party, but the fact is that you're NOT really ok. You've tried like the woman with the issue of blood in Mark 5 to get help, but you can't find any help at all. Because of your issues, you've begun to lose sight of just how valuable you are in the eyes of God, and you've begun to believe that things will never change. That's exactly where this woman was. Mark 5:25-34 says…

A woman who had had a hemorrhage for twelve years, and had endured much at the hands of many physicians, and had spent all that she had and was not helped at all, but rather had grown worse- after hearing about Jesus, she came up in the crowd behind Him and touched His cloak. For she thought, "If I just touch His garments, I will get well." Immediately the flow of her blood was dried up; and she felt in her body that she was healed of her affliction. Immediately Jesus, perceiving in Himself that the power proceeding from Him had gone forth, turned around in the crowd and said, "Who touched My garments?" And His disciples said to Him, "You see the crowd pressing in on You, and You say, 'Who touched Me?'" And He looked around to see the woman who had done this. But the woman fearing and trembling, aware of what had happened to her, came and fell down before Him and told Him the whole truth. And He said to her, "Daughter, your faith has made you well; go in peace and be healed of your affliction."

She probably felt worthless and hopeless. She was just ready to accept that it is what it is, and maybe, just maybe the physicians and everyone else are right. It's been like this for 12 years, it's probably going to be this way for another 12 years, maybe I should just get settled in and accept that this is just who I am. I wondered why our text says that she endured much at the hands of many physicians. I believe it was because…

1. The Woman was steadily reminded of her condition

In the Book of Leviticus 15:25-27 it says…

'If a woman has a discharge of blood for many days, other than at the time of her customary impurity, or if it runs beyond her usual time of impurity, all the days of her

unclean discharge shall be as the days of her customary impurity. She shall be unclean. Every bed on which she lies all the days of her discharge shall be to her as the bed of her impurity; and whatever she sits on shall be unclean, as the uncleanness of her impurity. Whoever touches those things shall be unclean; he shall wash his clothes and bathe in water, and be unclean until evening.

So based on what the scripture says I can imagine that for 12 years' physicians had been telling her that they can't help her and she's not getting any better. She went to the physicians, who were supposed to be able to help her, but they were probably more concerned about how her condition might affect them. I'm sure she kept being reminded of her hopeless condition every time she went to see a physician. One can only imagine the pain and emotional pressure that sapped her strength day after day. When you consider her many disappointments with the doctors and the poverty it brought her, you wonder how she endured as long as she did. Some of you reading this now, as you look back over the landscape of your life, and see that you are still dealing with the same thing now, you've asked yourself, how have I endured this so long. Your "so long" time may not be 12 years, yours might be 12 days, but for you, considering the situation, even that is just too long! She carried a heavy burden! This woman's affliction not only brought discomfort and discouragement, but it was embarrassing for it prevented her from worshiping at the temple (Lev. 15:19ff), she couldn't have normal social relationships, and she was treated almost as bad as a leper.

Perhaps some of you reading this have been going through something for a long time. You've been carrying a heavy burden. You've turned to family, friends, neighbors, co workers, and everyone you've turned to serves as a steady reminder of just how bad your situation seems to be. Rather than encourage you they remind you of your past as if it determines your present purpose, and they make judgments about your future, saying things won't change, because after all, it's been this way for so long. According to their assessment, you may as well just get settled in to your current condition, and stop looking for change, because change stopped being an option for you a long time ago. That reminds me to tell you that you've got to be careful who you choose to turn to for help. You've got to be careful who you award the title of friend. Some people you may think can help you are the very ones helping make things worse. Sometimes in order for change to happen **FOR** you change needs to happen **AROUND** you. Change your friends that always have something negative to say, change those people who want to control and manipulate you, change people who are always draining you with negativity and never making any positive deposits into you! This woman spent all she had! I know that when the text says that it's referring to all the money she spent, but she also spent something that some of you can identify with. She spent all of her emotional energy! She didn't know what else to do. All she tried for 12 years didn't work, so she probably felt like why keep trying the same thing and hoping for a different result. I'm out of money, getting worse, and emotionally drained. I guess my purpose in life is just to be a sick, hopeless, outcast of a woman with a dark, bleak future. I'll just settle for that I suppose. At least I tried. At least the doctors tried, but maybe this is just the hand I've been dealt in life. I'm just going to have to live with this issue. Maybe you're feeling like you're just going to have to live with certain issues. You've got a dead end job, a dead beat husband, or a broke boyfriend, friends have forsaken you, emotions are shattered, hormones out of whack, or you're battling sickness. Your theme song has become gloom, despair, and agony on me. Not only does it seem like there's no light at the end of the tunnel, it seems like the tunnel closed up a long time ago. Time will not allow me to list all of the possible issues you might be dealing with, but you can fill in the blank for yourself. What I do know is that you need to get what this woman got when she was at such a low point in her life. What did she get?

2. The Woman got a sudden revelation

In the midst of her despair, this woman who couldn't worship in the synagogues, couldn't have normal social relationships, was considered unclean, and was out of options got a sudden revelation! She somehow heard about a man named Jesus! We don't know how she heard, but I found it interesting that after 12 years and **many** physicians who couldn't help the **one** woman that her answer was found in the **One** who could help **many**! As I thought about this, I came up with three possible ways she heard...

- **Maybe she overheard somebody's conversation.**
- **Maybe she had one bold friend left that didn't care about people's perceptions that came and told her**

about Jesus.

- **Or, maybe people around her began to talk about Jesus because His travels brought Him close by.**

Based on the context of the verses preceding this text, and in light of this woman's weak, feeble condition, which made it very unlikely that she would be traveling anywhere, it seems that option 3 is the most likely scenario. When she heard about Him, faith rose up inside of her and caused her to believe that if she could just get close enough to touch His garment, this 12-year nightmare will be over! Matthew 11:28 says "Come unto me, all ye that labour and are heavy laden, and I will give you rest."

She didn't have much strength in her body, but when she heard of Jesus, something happened inside of her. For 12 long painful years this woman suffered, but when she heard about Jesus, faith rose up in her and she resolved within herself that she was going to press her way to Jesus!!! Sometimes you may feel like you don't have the strength to pray, you don't have the strength to go on any further, but when you hear the name of Jesus, something begins to happen inside of you and just like this woman you begin to press! In the midst of your situation, people may tell you, it will be alright, I'm praying for you. Sometimes though you reach the point of realizing that you need to press in for yourself! It's good to know people are praying for you and people have concern for you but you've got to have the spiritual tenacity that no matter what I've got to get a touch for myself! Thank you for your prayers, thank you for your concern, but I've got to press in and get my touch! I don't know how far this woman had to go to join in the crowd and get her touch, but her mind was made up that 12 years has been long enough, and I'm pressing in for my touch today!!! She pressed through the pain, pressed through the despair, pressed through the hopelessness, pressed through the discouragement, pressed through the crowd because she heard about Jesus! She could have spent the rest of her life feeling sorry for herself and wondering why she had to go through like this. She could have used any number of excuses to convince herself to stay away from Him. She might have said: "I'm not important enough to ask Jesus for help!" or "Look, He's going with Jairus, so I won't bother Him now." She could have argued that nothing else had helped her, so why try again? Or she might have concluded that it was not right to come to Jesus as a last resort, after visiting all those physicians. However, she laid aside all arguments and excuses and came by faith to Jesus. Because of her uncleanness, she wasn't even supposed to be in the crowd. She heard what the doctor's said, what people said, she probably even started talking bad about herself, but she heard about Jesus, and nothing was going to stop her **that day** from getting her touch! Seeing her resolve to get close to Jesus reminded me that what you hear has a direct impact on the actions you take! Her actions show that she was acting in faith. She had no evidence that she would get what she wanted. She had no friends coming to report what they experienced themselves. All she did was heard about Jesus. I want to ask you the question, **"What have you heard?"** You've heard what's been said about you in the past. You've heard the negative reports from friends, family, neighbors, or even people that don't even like you, concerning your situation. You've heard what the devil has managed to plant in your mind about your situation. But in case you haven't heard, or maybe you just need to be reminded, Jesus is a way maker, Jesus is a healer, Jesus is a deliverer, and Jesus is everything you need!!! If you didn't know now you know and if you just got off focus get your eyes back on Jesus, the author and finisher of our faith!

An interesting fact that jumped out at me was THE STORY NEVER SAYS THAT THE WOMAN DID ANYTHING TO DESERVE HER SITUATION. SOME OF YOU MAY BE WONDERING WHY YOU HAVE HAD TO GO THROUGH. Just like this woman, you probably even asked the famous question, WHY ME?

I want to tell you, that there is good news! You don't have to be stuck where you are! You can get your blessing now but you've got to press in to Jesus! You've got to have the determination that no matter who or what tries to get in my way, I'm going to press in for my blessing! You've got to have faith to believe that something is going to change for you! She was constantly reminded of her condition, she got a sudden revelation, and she was…

3. Supernaturally Released

The woman got her healing IMMEDIATELY. It wasn't 12 more seconds, 12 more minutes, 12 more weeks, 12 more months or 12 more years, it was, RIGHT NOW!!! No matter how bad your situation may be, and no matter how long you've been in it, you can get your healing, your breakthrough, your deliverance, RIGHT NOW!!! You can experience SUPERNATURAL RELEASE now!!! Your emotions can be made whole, your physical body can be made whole, your marriage and family relationships can be made whole, your mind can be made whole, and it can take place RIGHT NOW!!! How can it happen? It is according to your FAITH.

Faith operates beyond reason. For example, Noah built an ark, which made no sense to others, but it saved his life and lives of his family. The three Hebrew boys, rather than bow down to the king, were thrown in the fiery furnace. When the king looked in he said I thought we threw in 3 but I see a 4th and he looks like the son of God. Daniel was thrown in the lion's den, but rather than be devoured, he was unharmed because God moved on his behalf. Faith cannot be rationalized. Faith cannot be explained. You've just got to have faith. Just like God made the unreasonable happen for this woman, He can do the same for you but you've got to press in by faith!!!

What many Christians call faith is really faith in their own reasoning skills. You may never hear a believer verbalize it this way, but faith in your own reasoning skills is this... as soon as I can make sense of how this is going to happen and how it can benefit me, **THEN** I will act. Too many believers are trying to operate in faith with their head and believe in something that their mind cannot wrap itself around. That would be ok if Hebrews 11:1 said...*Now faith is the substance of things I'm able to rationalize and the evidence of things which I clearly see.* However, we know that the word of God actually says in Hebrews 11:1-3... *Now faith is the substance of things hoped for, the evidence of things not seen. For by it (faith) the elders obtained a good testimony. By faith we understand that the worlds were <u>framed by the word of God</u>, so that the things which are seen were <u>not made of things which are visible</u>.*

In order for you to walk in faith, you have to frame your life by the word of God. Get rid of words of doubt, negativity and unbelief and start saying what God's word says, and you'll tap in to the supernatural realm and see the blessings of God manifest.

Because of her faith, she was made whole! She elbowed her way through the crowd, determined to get her breakthrough regardless of what people thought and said. But she wanted to go unnoticed. The question may be asked, "Why?" Simply because this was a personal, embarrassing matter that she wanted to keep secret. The woman planned to slip away and get lost in the crowd, but Jesus turned and stopped her. She wanted to get her blessing but she did not want anyone to know. That's how some of you might do. But after God brings you out, let Him use you!!! She did not want to share the testimony of how she had a problem for so long and how Jesus made her whole. There may have been some there who were not aware of her former condition, and if they heard her testimony, they may have ridiculed her.

This woman wasn't even supposed to be in the crowd, but that's what faith will do. It will take you places other people may say you don't belong. Society wrote this woman off and had already given their final verdict on her, but she had faith! Faith took her from I'm finished, to I'm focused. Faith took her from where she was, to where she needed to be. When Jesus called her out, I'm sure there were people in the crowd that recognized who she was and said how did she get here? We thought she was done, we thought she was going to die, but here she is! How did she do it, BY FAITH!

People will talk about you too. When they know you're going through something and having some issues and they'll write you off. They'll pass judgment on you and their verdict will be that you are finished, and then all of a sudden, there you are! They'll say things like I know she was having issues, I know her husband was no good, I know she lost that job, I know she was abused, I know she was abandoned by her family, so how did she get here!!! Your testimony will also be that it was BY FAITH!!!

Jesus asked the question, "Who touched me?" There was a supernatural release at the moment of that touch. The disciples were somewhat surprised at Jesus' question. He was completely surrounded by a mass of people. In their surprise, they asked Him why He was asking such a question in the midst of so many people. How could He possibly expect not to be touched?

The woman confessed. When Jesus asked the question, the woman came up to Jesus "fearing and trembling." She had approached Him being unclean and had not requested permission to touch Him. But she had still been healed. She feared that somehow her healing might be reversed if she did not confess that she had touched Him. So *"knowing what was done in her, she came and fell down before Him, and told Him all the truth."* It was difficult and embarrassing, but she did it. There were many others in that crowd who were close to Jesus and even pressing against Him, but they experienced no miracles. Why? It was because they did not have faith. Why did He not simply permit her to remain anonymous and go her way? Jesus dealt with her publicly that she might have the opportunity to share her testimony and glorify the Lord. This woman recognized that she needed to touch Jesus, and Jesus used her to touch the people with her testimony. The same woman that nobody wanted to touch and didn't want her to touch them, was now the one touching them all. Psalms 107 tells us ***"Let the redeemed of the Lord say so, whom He hath redeemed from the hand of the enemy.... He sent His word, and healed them.... Oh, that men would praise the Lord for His goodness, and for His wonderful works to the children of men!"*** She was healed and the same can happen for you. It doesn't matter how bad your situation is, your faith can make you whole. Just press in, reach out and touch God now. Imagine for a moment if the woman believed, but that was it. Imagine if she would have just started having a desire to touch His garment, but never acted upon that. There would have been no victory in her situation. Why? Because victory is never celebrated in the starting blocks, victory is obtained by the press. I've never seen a gold medal awarded at the starting line, it's always after the finish. The apostle Paul said in Philippians 3:14...

Brethren, I count not myself to have apprehended: but this one thing I do, forgetting those things which are behind, and reaching forth unto those things which are before, I press toward the mark for the prize of the high calling of God in Christ Jesus.

Your life may seem broken, but God can put it back together again. In order for you to experience Supernatural release, you've got to release your faith and once you receive your blessing, you must realize that you now have a story to share and respect yourself enough to know that YOUR story is worth telling!

You must receive the revelation, retrieve your identity, remain focused on the King's perspective of you, and realize your story has value. Many women, even after what they've already read here, will still struggle to find the value in their story or in themselves. Here is a story I read that I believe will encourage you...

Suppose that during the past week a young wife gave birth to her first baby. Now suppose that as she held her new baby in her arms and was enjoying the pleasure of motherhood, someone came up to her and said, "How much do you want for the child?" Of course she would show no interest in the offer and would be offended at even a suggestion that her precious babe was for sale. But the stranger is persistent and offers ten thousand dollars, then a hundred thousand dollars, and finally one million dollars. The offers are in vain because the mother will simply press the baby closer to her and reply, "My baby is worth more to me than the entire world!"

Of course, if she didn't say that, we would question whether she had the proper attitude for motherhood. But why does she say it? Is it because she looks forward to thousands of dirty diapers, sleepless nights with a sick child, and the costs of raising that child? Is it because the child will bring her fame and fortune? Of course not. Rather, it is because she has chosen to value this tiny person, to deem the small one to be of worth, and to love that baby of hers. Such worth resides in the very identity of a person, not in their performance, and such worth, coming from the image of

God in all of us, must be the basis for our concept of ourselves, if our self portrait is to be durable and worthwhile.

You have worth! You have the image of God in you! Your self portrait is durable and worthwhile! Respect yourself, let God use you to fulfill the destiny He has for you, and share your testimony to help others turn to God and get the help they need!!!

Chapter Five
Refuse to Compromise Who You Are

Over the past 50 years or so, there has been a serious moral decline in our country. Right truly is being called wrong and wrong truly is being called right. In fact, some people say there is no such thing as an absolute right anymore. If it feels good to you it must be right in spite of others who may call it wrong. We used to have a reverence and respect for the bible and for the things of God, but now people have more respect for the temporal things of the world rather than the eternal things of God. People who were once zealous and on fire for God have cooled off because they have believed the lies of people who say it's not necessary to be so committed. "Have some fun", they say. They don't realize that you can have the most fun when you have totally devoted yourself to God. In an ever increasing effort to satisfy self, man has become bolder at engaging in things that in the past would have been widely recognized as sinful. The word sin isn't even heard much anymore, even in the church. It's as if man has turned their backs on God and said *"God, we don't care what your way says, our way is much better. We want our satisfaction now! We want our reward now; we want our fulfillment now! Your way God is not good enough! In fact, your way is not even the best way anymore! We have figured out something better. After we are done here on Earth, then we will have time for You when we get to Heaven. Right now, it's about what we want! Oh, if we run into any trouble, we will send up a prayer. Well, got to go, talk to you later God."* Not only does it seem like God's standards have been rejected by the non Christians, but it appears to have been rejected in many ways by Christians too! There used to be a time when abstinence was the accepted norm to prevent children born out of wedlock, but now its abortion. There was a time when sex outside of marriage was taboo, but now it's not taboo it's considered the thing to do. Marriage was accepted as one man and one woman but now people say, "Well I guess if Joe and Steve want to be together, that's ok. It's nobody else's business" Television used to be something that was safe to allow your kids to watch UNSUPERVISED! Now, it's not only unsafe to allow your kids to watch unsupervised, but as an adult, you can barely watch TV without hearing profanity, having lustful innuendo showered on you, seeing people in situations of fornication and adultery and more. These things used to be banned from TV but now they are approved all in the name of building the storyline and promoting creativity. Lust is being called love and love is assumed to be sex. In today's world if you say I love you to someone people automatically assume there's more to it. Assumption, however, is the lowest form of knowledge. This moral decline has given birth to so many illicit things and one that is such a phenomenon now that it has its own movie is a thing called friends with benefits. These relationships happen to Christians and non Christians because of the belief in the lie that they must do this to keep the relationship going. If you are a Christian, it is better to obey God than to satisfy the sexual desires in the relationship. If you are not a Christian, it is better to abstain too. What is the world's view of a friend with benefits? The idea of friends with benefits relationship from a worldly perspective is that two friends set out to have a sexual relationship without being emotionally involved. It is the idea of two good friends who have casual sex *without a monogamous relationship* or any kind of commitment. That means if they are getting "benefits" from you, they are probably getting "benefits" from others too. My mother once told someone the vagina is a treasure and you should not give your treasure to everyone. That's a bold statement, but it's a dose of truth more need to hear which is why I included it in this book. Thanks mom!

Friends with benefits is really not new, it's just been given a palatable title now so that it will be seen as socially acceptable. There are several problems with this twisted thinking process. I'll share a few God showed me…

1. **God never intended sex to be a casual recreational activity.** He does not consent, which makes it wrong outside the boundaries of marriage no matter how consenting the two individuals may be. That goes for Christians and non Christians alike. (Exodus 20:14 and Galatians5:19,21)

2. **A person in a FWB relationship is living in SIN.** Sin is a word that is rarely used in the 21st century where relativism, humanism, selfishness and apathy towards the things of God are running rampant, while at the same time destroying the principles of morality and decency that once were the norm in

society.

3. **In a friend with benefits relationship someone always gets hurt.** The man and woman can be emotionally scarred because each is being seen as an object of pleasure and not as a person worthy of being committed to in marriage. When either has emotions that desire more than an FWB relationship, they are hurt by the response from a person who only wants a physical not emotional bond. Many, though, have argued that non-marriage sex is not all that harmful.

The physical consequences are becoming increasingly obvious and increasingly dangerous in today's society. Someone once said AIDS and other Sexually Transmitted Diseases are frightening realities. "Safe sex" is more accurately described as "reduced risk sex." The only truly safe sex is abstinence. There is also a very real risk that children could be born — and possibly grow up without two parents. Your actions affect your life, your partner's life, and the lives of your family. They can result in handicapping an innocent baby's life as well. Worst of all the willful destruction of human life often results from pre-marital sex.

The relational consequences are just as real, though they may be more difficult to grasp.

First, sin always damages a person's relationship with God. Psalm 66:18 says, *"If I had cherished sin in my heart, the Lord would not have listened."* Intentional disobedience of God's command to not commit adultery, fornicate, or any other sinful behavior dishonors and displeases God. God is pleased when His children choose obedience and self-control instead of the immediacy of pleasure.

Secondly, relational damage happens between a Christian and those who are watching his or her life. For example, the sin of adultery causes a person's friends and even "outsiders" to view the adulterer as less committed to obedience, and more prone to hypocrisy. But a Christian who saves himself or herself in obedience to God wins the respect of those who see his or her life.

Thirdly, Sex outside of marriage also damages the relationship between the persons involved. Trust is the main issue here. If two people do not cherish sex enough to wait for a marriage commitment, how can they trust one another for fidelity? A man and woman build trust and respect for one another when they both survive the struggles of self-control — each will have the confidence that the other respects them, and cherishes their intimacy. Some married couples allow each other to have sex with other people. These people are called swingers. People in these relationships, just like Friends with Benefits, are living in sin and need deliverance.

Too many people enter friendships with a "what's in it for me" mentality. Joe O'Day, author of <u>The Art of Friendship</u>, writes, **"Our preoccupation is usually with <u>having</u> friends. The Bible's focus is on <u>being</u> a friend."** Another problem is that the society we live in has gotten so far away from what is decent and respectful and right, that they really don't understand what a friend actually is. The key problem with a friend with benefits mentality is lust. People lust for things that they want and develop ways to satisfy their lusts even if it means there is harm that will come to them. When a person lusts for something, they aren't concerned about the harm, they want what they want. Calling the relationship, a "friends with benefits" relationship, is an attempt to make something wrong right by giving it a catchy title. No matter how catchy the title, it is still SIN, and therefore, it is wrong.

Lust is the beginning of a process to carry out sin! The Book of James described this process in Chapter 1:14-15. What he shows is a four step process in how sin is carried out. He says:

But each one is tempted when he is carried away and enticed by his own lust. Then when lust has conceived, it gives birth to sin; and when sin is accomplished, it brings forth death.

The Bible Exposition Commentary explains the four step process...

1. Desire (v. 14). The word *lust* means any kind of desire, and not necessarily sexual passions. The normal desires of life were given to us by God and, of themselves, are not sinful. Without these desires, we could not function. Unless we felt hunger and thirst, we would never eat and drink, and we would die. It is when we want to satisfy these desires in ways outside God's will that we get into trouble.

2. Deception (v. 14). Temptation always carries with it some bait that appeals to our natural desires. The bait not only attracts us, but it also hides the fact that yielding to the desire will eventually bring sorrow and punishment.

The bait keeps us from seeing the consequences of sin.

3. Disobedience (v. 15). We have moved from the *emotions* (desire) and the *intellect* (deception) to the *will*. James changed the picture from hunting and fishing to the birth of a baby. Desire conceives a method for taking the bait. The will approves and acts; and the result is sin. Whether we feel it or not, we are hooked and trapped. The more you exercise your will in saying a decisive no to temptation, the more God will take control of your life. *"for it is **God who works in you both to will and to do for [His] good pleasure."** (Phil. 2:13).*

4. Death (v. 15). Disobedience gives birth to death, not life. It may take years for the sin to mature, but when it does, the result will be death. If we will only believe God's Word and see this final tragedy, it will encourage us not to yield to temptation. Friends with benefits relationships should really be called enemies with disadvantages relationships because a friend who will join you in sin is not a friend with benefits.

There ought to be some benefits in a friendship, just not the so called benefits that are being promoted by our society.

Do not take the devil's bait and think that you must allow yourself to compromise who you are and end up in this or any similar kind of relationship. Now that we know what we should not do, let's look at what a real friend with benefits relationship should look like.

Chapter Six
Resolve to have Godly Boundaries

What is a real friend with benefits relationship? This is important to know as you build a healthy respect for yourself and maintain a Godly perspective of you. Having this knowledge can affect how you present yourself to others. How you present yourself is how you will be received. If you present yourself as an easy target, that's how you will be received. However, if you present yourself as a person that commands respect, you will be received that way. Not only should you look for these benefits in a relationship with a potential husband, but you should provide these benefits as well. These qualities are not only applicable in the case of a potential husband, but these also apply to female friendships. As you look at these you may realize that there are not only some male friends you need to rid yourself of, but there are probably some female friends you need to break free from. If you want to become the woman God made you to be, it's wise to surround yourself with women who have that same desire. If you surround yourself with women who show they are not committed to obeying God, you may find yourself being led to act the same way they do. Do your female friends gossip? Do they dress provocatively? Do they see nothing wrong with hooking up with a guy every now and then? Do they treat their husbands like garbage? Are they selfish? Do they get defensive as soon as you give them constructive criticism? Are they always complaining and being negative about something every time you talk to them? Are they unfaithful in church attendance? There are many more examples I can use here, but if you have a friend like this, you should rethink that friendship. If you don't, before you know it, you'll probably start feeling like there's nothing wrong with these things too. In Proverbs 12:26 (NKJV) it says... ***The righteous should choose his friends carefully, for the way of the wicked leads them astray.*** I used the word FRIEND as an acronym for these six benefits to make them easy to remember.

1. **The Benefit of Fellowship-** According to Got Questions Ministries, The principle of friendship is also found in Amos. *"Can two walk together, unless they are agreed?"*

(Amos 3:3 NKJV). Friends are of like mind. The truth that comes from all of this is a friendship is a relationship that is entered into by individuals, and it is only as good or as close as those individuals choose to make it. Someone has said that if you can count your true friends on the fingers of one hand, you are blessed. A friend is one whom you can be yourself with and never fear that he or she will judge you. A friend is someone that you can confide in with complete trust. A friend is someone you respect and that respects you, not based upon worthiness but based upon a likeness of mind.

2. **The Benefit of Restoration-** *"A friend loves at all times, and a brother is born for adversity"* **(Proverbs 17:17).** Friendship is at its best not in times of prosperity and ease, but in times of trouble. Friendship has to be constant. Friends don't leave you when you are going through tough times. If you have made a mistake or had some moral failure in your life, your friends will not gather the facts and talk about you as they are leaving you. Your friends will talk to you and find out how to plan a strategy for you to make a comeback! Maybe the

business plan failed. Maybe the marriage didn't work; maybe you lied or stole something. You need friends that will ride out the tough times with you! That verse literally means that in tough times a friend that loves at all times becomes a brother in adversity. While others are jumping ship and walking away from you, they stay right there with you! You already feel bad enough when you've made a mistake, you don't need to surround yourself with people that will constantly remind you of what you did!

3. **The Benefit of Intimacy**- You can have an intimate relationship with a friend but that is not the same thing as a sexual relationship. The world has totally confused the terms. Having an intimate relationship means that you have a deeper knowledge of who they are. You don't just know the things that a general acquaintance would know, but you know them on a more personal level.

You know their faults, weaknesses, mistakes, goals, and they know yours, but it is not a sexually intimate relationship. It is a friendship.

4. **The Benefit of Encouragement-** They will encourage you to <u>do right</u>. *"Wounds from a friend can be trusted, but an enemy multiplies kisses" (Proverbs 27:6).*

According to Pastor Dave McFadden, at least two things are being said to us in this verse. **First, a true friend is honest** - *"Wounds from a friend"*. 84 times the Gospels record Jesus saying *"I tell you the truth."* Jesus didn't hesitate to speak the truth and neither should we if we are a true friend. A true friend is willing, if need be, to confront you with the sometimes "painful truth." H or she is willing to tell you what you need to hear in order to help you. A true friend shares his honesty out of a spirit of concern, not a spirit of criticism! He seeks to follow Ephesians 4:15, to *'speak the truth in love."* Therefore, he will combine truth with tenderness.

You see, truthfulness without tenderness is to be calloused. Tenderness without truthfulness is to be cowardly. But truthfulness with tenderness is to be Christian! **Second, a true friend is helpful** - *"Wounds from a friend can be trusted"*

A true friend wants you to…

A**. Receive the best** - A personal & growing relationship with God.
B. **Believe the best** - A perspective on life only God can give.
C. **Achieve the best** - Potential that God alone can help us achieve.

They will also encourage you when you seem tired of situations in life or ready to quit pursuing something you've been trying to achieve for a long time, your friend will put you in remembrance of the potential in you. They will remind you of the goals you set and help steer you back on the right path!

5. **The Benefit of Nobility-** What is nobility? It is the state or quality of being morally or spiritually good. **They will not influence you to join them in sin.** They are committed to righteousness. Paul told the church at Corinth some very important information regarding this very thing. He said in 1 Corinthians 5:11 *But now I have written to you not to keep company with anyone named a brother, who is sexually immoral, or covetous, or an idolater, or a reviler, or a drunkard, or an extortioner-- not even to eat with such a person.* In 1 Cor 15:33 I believe he gives the very reason why we should observe this instruction when he said *"Do not be deceived: "Bad company corrupts good morals."* I read a story about a farmer, troubled by a flock of crows in his corn field, which loaded his shotgun and crawled unseen along the fence-row, determined to get a shot at the crows. Now the farmer had a very "sociable" parrot that made friends with *everybody*. Seeing the flock of crows, the parrot flew over and joined them (just being sociable). The farmer saw the crows, but didn't see the parrot. He took careful aim at the crows and BANG!!! He shot them. The farmer crawled over the fence to pick up the fallen crows, and to

his surprise there was the parrot, badly ruffled, with a broken wing but still alive. The farmer carried the parrot home, where his children met him. Seeing that their pet was injured, they tearfully asked, "What happened papa?" Before he could answer the parrot spoke up and said, "Bad Company!" The lesson to us is that we must watch the company we keep!

6. **The Benefit of Devotion** - A real friend knows that the relationship is really not about them, but what they can do for you. Seeking another person's highest good: that's being a true friend. The Bible says in John chapter 15 *"Greater love has no one than this, than to lay down one's life for his friends."* If a person is only there for you in good times, then they are just a fair weather acquaintance and not a friend at all.

Those benefits are good news, but there is more good news! If you are in a relationship, whether it's a friends with benefits relationship where you are being taken advantage of, or an adulterous relationship, fornication, or any other relationship that is not pleasing to God and you know in your own God given conscience that it is not right, I know a friend who is able to deliver you out of that and any other situation. He is the best of friends and His name is Jesus! Everybody should have a friend like Jesus, and the good news is that everybody can! A man named Henry Bosch once said Socrates taught for 40 years, Plato for 50, Aristotle for 40, and Jesus for only 3. Yet the influence of His 3-year ministry infinitely transcends the impact left by the combined 130 years of teaching from these men who were among the greatest philosophers of all time. Jesus painted no pictures; yet, some of the finest paintings of Raphael, Michelangelo, and Leonardo da Vinci received their inspiration from Him. Jesus wrote no poetry; but Dante, Milton, and scores of the world's greatest poets were inspired by Him. Jesus composed no music; still Haydn, Handel, Beethoven, Bach, and Mendelssohn reached their highest perfection of melody in the hymns, symphonies, and oratories they composed in His praise. Every sphere of human greatness has been enriched by this humble Carpenter of Nazareth.

The Lord Jesus Christ gave us the definition of a true friend: *"Greater love has no one than this that he lay down his life for his friends. You are my friends if you do what I command. I no longer call you servants, because a servant does not know his master's business. Instead, I have called you friends, for everything that I learned from my Father I have made known to you" (John 15:13-15).* Jesus is the best example of a true friend, for He laid down His life for His "friends." What is more, anyone may become His friend by trusting in Him as his personal savior, being born again and receiving new life in Him.

Ralph Waldo Emerson said: "The only way to have a friend is to be one." A friend is one who is a source of sunshine when you are under the weather. A friend is one who believes in you, when you cease to believe in yourself. A friend is a source of celebration when you feel that there is nothing to celebrate. A friend is one who answers your call before you call. Friendship is of two categories. It is first vertical or God-ward and second horizontal or a reaching outward. Friendship thrives upon sacrifice. You can give without love but you cannot love without giving. True friendship is when two friends can walk in opposite directions, and yet remain side by side.

A friend is one who walks in when the rest of the world walks out. A friendship with Jesus is truly the only unsinkable-ship.

Jesus is that friend that sticks closer than a brother. Even the best of friends can let you down at times, but Jesus will never let you down. He never leaves nor forsakes you. He is the epitome of a friend who will have fellowship with you, restore you, and the intimacy you can have with Him cannot be compared to any other. He will encourage you, and he is the noblest of all! He is so devoted to you that even before you could call yourself a friend He died for you! Some of you have had friends betray you, deceive you, take advantage of you, and you may be saying I need healing. Jesus is the healer. Some of you have been seeking fulfillment in all sorts of things and have been left feeling empty. Jesus is that fulfillment you need. Some of you in the economic climate we live in are looking for peace of mind and cannot find it, but He will give you peace that passes all understanding. Maybe you've done some things you wouldn't want anyone to know about, and you can't imagine coming to Jesus with all that guilt and shame. I want you to know Jesus already knows what you did, and loves you anyway and is waiting on you to come to Him! He knows your struggle and He is the master of giving second chances. Maybe you started a relationship with Jesus, and you've strayed away. He's waiting on your return to Him with open arms! Perhaps you have been running from a relationship with Jesus and you now realize that the relationship you've been running from is the one you really need. The best Friend with the greatest benefits is Jesus and He is waiting on you.

Chapter Seven
Recognize God's Man for You

Many of you reading this have a desire to be married but the right man has not come along yet. Some men may have come along that were the devils counterfeit, and you were duped into a relationship thinking that this was God's doing, only to realize later that you were not hearing the voice of God, but the voice of your own flesh. Far too much of what people attribute to God speaking to them really is them operating in the flesh. Having a desire to be married is fine, but you must also be sure that you are a person a man would want to be married to. You've got to have more to offer than a pretty smile, nice figure, or whatever other external attribute that would catch the man's eye. You've got to strive to be God's woman before God's man can really consider you his "good thing". Proverbs 18:22 says...*He who finds a wife finds a good thing and obtains favor from the LORD.* Please note that it says he FINDS THE WIFE. God's man is not going to be attracted to the woman who is putting all her assets on display as she is trying to find the man. Modesty in your attire is attractive. If you respect yourself and are trying to become the woman God made you to be, you will understand the power of modesty. **How you present yourself is how you will be received.** If you want a man to approach you in a respectful way, then look like someone who commands respect. If you want to look like a loose woman who is having sex with whosoever will come, then that's what you'll attract. God's woman is modest, and she will attract God's man. For those of you that are already married, this chapter will be great information to share with young women who are about to make a bad decision to enter into a relationship with the wrong guy or for those women who seem to have a propensity for getting hooked up with the wrong guy again and again and again. This last chapter is a practical guide to help you identify GOD'S MAN and avoid the mistake so many women make of settling for whoever shows some kind of interest in them, and calling it God's will, even though the man has exhibited numerous signs to contradict that. Don't get desperate and settle for whoever comes along!!! If you have a solid relationship with Jesus, you won't get desperate; you will wait and recognize God's man for you! Ladies, stop rushing into relationships so fast! Let the man prove he is worthy of you first before you rush to Facebook to change your relationship status! Otherwise, you may simply end up being another notch in his belt as he moves on to find the next victim.

God's man for you will exhibit the following qualities. Don't neglect these qualities for in doing so you could have a lifetime of regret. I have used the acronym HUSBAND to help you remember these valuable points.

A potential husband will...

1. **Have a relationship with God** – This cannot be a superficial relationship! In other words, he needs to show **definite proof** of a relationship with God before you declare the two of you to be in relationship. 2 Corinthians 6:14-15 says...*Do not be bound together with unbelievers; for what partnership have righteousness and lawlessness, or what fellowship has light with darkness? Or what harmony has Christ with Belial, or what has a believer in common with an unbeliever?* I have seen so many women (and men) over the years settle for someone because

they looked good on the outside, said nice things to them, got them pregnant, etc, but they overlook the first quality that qualifies them for a deeper relationship, and that is having a relationship with God. Just for clarity, you should be born again and have a real relationship with God too. I think you've been able to make that assumption so far in this book. God's man won't just talk about church; he will be actively going to a church that he is a member of. He won't just talk about scriptures; he will apply them. He will have a prayer life. He will have a pastor than can vouch for how genuine his relationship with God is. He will have friends who can vouch for his commitment to God. His salvation won't be something that you are still unsure about after a few weeks. If you are, then he's probably not God's man for you. If you are thinking that you will change him after you compromise and start a relationship with him, then you have just told him by your actions that you are fine with the way he is and that there is no reason for him to change. Therefore, the likelihood of you changing him by leading him to receiving Christ is not impossible, but the odds are not in your favor. He needs to have a solid relationship with God first before he ever lays eyes on you. However, finding someone in a church service is no guarantee that he or she is a Christian. Only examining that person and prayer will help to determine if the person is really a Christian or not. The signs that he is will be just as obvious as the signs that say he is not.

2. **Understand Commitment –** He will understand that marriage is a relationship that requires commitment, and he needs to show a commitment to you before any engagement ring is purchased. If he is dating you and flirting with other women too, he's not committed. He is really a player who is trying to get as much play as he can. If you keep catching him texting inappropriate messages to other women, looking at the half naked or completely naked pictures they have sent him, and people keep telling you they keep seeing him leaving other women's houses saying he was just there to help them with

some household chores, he's not the one for you. Stop accepting his, "baby I'm sorry" excuses and start realizing he actually is a SORRY MAN who is wasting your time! Open your eyes and see this is not a man God would send you! If he is like this now and you get engaged to him, unless some drastic changes are made such as him giving his life to Jesus, he will be a player even after the "I do's" too. What I really want you to understand about the commitment he must have is that it must be a commitment to God **FIRST**. 1 Kings 8:61 says… *Let your heart therefore be wholly devoted to the* LORD *our God, to walk in His statutes and to keep His commandments, as at this day.* Before you can expect him to be committed to you, you should set a standard that he MUST be committed to God; not just saved, but committed.

3. **Support your dreams and goals** – You certainly ought to have some dreams and goals for your life. The man who meets this list of qualities should encourage you and support you towards achieving those goals. If he is discouraging you and showing

no interest in your ambitions, that is not a good sign. 1 Peter 3:7 says… ***You husbands in the same way, live with your wives in an understanding way, as with someone weaker, since she is a woman; and <u>show her honor</u> as a fellow heir of the grace of life, so that your prayers will not be hindered.*** When this verse says show her honor, it does not mean that the man is going to give in to you and do whatever you say. As the spiritual leader in the home, he may disagree with you on some things while at the same time respecting you. However, giving honor does mean that the man will give consideration to your dreams, goals, feelings, desires and thoughts. **Before** the man becomes a husband to you, he should exhibit this quality.

4. **Bring something to the table** – What does he have to offer you? Can you see yourself committing to marry this man? If he is overly connected to mama and daddy, seeking their advice on matters that the two of you should discuss amongst yourselves, or if he is grown, living with his parents still, and has zero ambition to accomplish anything or get his own place,

he is probably not what you're looking for. If he has no skills that lead to employment, cannot have an intelligent discussion with you about anything other than sports, has baby mamas all over the country, can't keep a job or any money, he's probably not what you're looking for. Pay attention to the obvious red flags!!! Get to know their character before you commit to a relationship with them. On that note, **you** should also be bringing something to the table. Examine yourself. What do you offer that would make God's man interested in being with you? Notice I said God's man and not just any man. God's man is going to have something to offer and he's going to be looking for what you have to offer. Remember, in Proverbs 18:22 the bible says… *He who finds a wife finds a good thing and obtains favor from the LORD.* Before you start desiring a husband, make sure you have the qualities of a wife. What are those qualities? Look at what Proverbs 31:10-31 says… *<u>An excellent wife</u>, who can find? For her worth is far above jewels. The heart of her husband trusts in her, and he will have no lack of gain. She does him good and not evil all the days of her life. She looks for wool and flax* *and works with her hands in delight. She is like merchant ships; she brings her food from afar. She rises also while it is still night and gives food to her household and portions to her maidens. She considers a field and buys it; from her earnings she plants a vineyard. She girds herself with strength and makes her arms strong. She senses that her gain is good; her lamp does not go out at night. She stretches out her hands to the distaff, and her hands grasp the spindle. She extends her hand to the poor, and she stretches out her hands to the needy. She is not afraid of the snow for her household, for all her household are clothed with scarlet. She makes coverings for herself; her clothing is fine linen and purple. Her husband is known in the gates, when he sits among the elders of the land. She makes linen garments and sells them, and supplies belts to the tradesmen. Strength and dignity are her clothing, and she smiles at the future. She opens her mouth in wisdom, and the teaching of kindness is on her tongue. She looks well to the ways of her household, and does not eat the bread of idleness. Her children rise up and bless her; her husband also, and he praises her, saying: "Many daughters have done nobly, but you excel them all." Charm is deceitful and beauty is vain, but a woman who fears the LORD, she shall be praised. Give her the product of her hands, and let her works praise her in the gates.*

There is much debate over whether a wife is to exhibit ALL of these qualities, but there is no reason why a woman couldn't exhibit many or all of them. If you notice, there is nothing in the passage of scripture in Proverbs 31 that indicates that a wife would not be able to have all these qualities. Another thing to take note of is that this is coming from THE WORD OF GOD. If you want to be the woman God made you to be, then embrace what the word of God is saying. Personally, I believe I am truly married to a Proverbs 31 woman who does exhibit all of these qualities. If you want to be all that God made you to be, you will want to have more to offer than good looks, and if your skills are lacking, you CAN and SHOULD change that. As a woman with a healthy respect for herself, you should want a man to recognize that he is in the presence of a woman of substance; a wife, not just another woman! If he just wants a woman, he can find that anywhere. You have to make him realize you are on another level. Now, I am not saying that you absolutely MUST HAVE every single quality Proverbs 31 lists, but I am definitely saying that you should be described by several of those qualities if you are becoming the woman God made you to be. As I said before, how you present yourself is how you will be received. Listen, I am a man and I KNOW men want you to look good, but they want to know that there's some substance to go along with your good looks. Can you cook? Do you like to keep a clean household? Do you have good money management? If you don't have anything to offer but good looks, he is probably not going to be interested in being anything more than your friend unless he is desperate. Let me also add that I believe that a man should be able to cook, clean, manage money, etc, as well. He may not be a chef or anything, and neither may you, but knowing these basic things is critical for survival. When a person leaves their parents house, they have to be able to eat! You can't eat out all the time. It isn't wise to do so, and it's expensive to eat out all the time. If you don't know how to cook, that's no excuse because YOU CAN LEARN. My wife is a prime example of that. Her mother did not teach her to cook; she taught herself and she is an excellent cook. If you don't know how to clean, YOU CAN LEARN. If you're bad with managing your money, YOU CAN LEARN. Do you see the recurring theme here? As I said earlier, if your skills are lacking, you CAN and SHOULD change that. Find a woman who knows how to do these things and let her mentor you, but don't waste their time. If you want to learn, listen to what they are trying to teach you and apply it. If you are truly a "good thing", what is on the inside is going to be much more valuable than what is on the outside. The external attributes can change. If you have a baby, for example, you could have weight on you that may take a long time to go away and may never go away. If the outside is all he was interested in, then your relationship is in jeopardy as soon as the baby is conceived. Likewise, you should have this same mindset in regards to him. If good looks are all that he's bringing to the table, you can find that elsewhere in the man that IS actually bringing something to the table. Some of the questions you should get answers to are…Is he employed? Does he have a desire to be successful in life? Does he have dreams and goals? What are those dreams and goals? Are we compatible? How was he raised as a child? What kind of relationship do his mother and father have? **Before you marry the man you both should get premarital counseling.** If he's not bringing anything to the table, stay available for the man who will find you that does have something to offer.

5. **Always look out for your best interest –** The word of God tells us in Ephesians 5:25 says… *Husbands, love your wives, just as Christ also loved the church and gave Himself up for her.* He must display this before a serious relationship ensues. My beautiful wife, Valerie, tells people of the time before we were married, when she was stranded on her way back from Houston, TX, and she called me for help. Her

car broke down and she had no way to get back home which was still about two hours away. I had to be at the church I attended to unlock the building and serve, and I could easily have said that I could not help her, but I didn't say that. In fact, I drove all that way, late at night, to pick her, a female friend of hers and her son up, and I did not have any ulterior motive. I simply wanted her to be safe, and I allowed her to use another vehicle I owned until she could get hers repaired. Her father told her that if a man shows that he loves you more than he loves himself, then he is probably the one for you. I guess I passed the test! Her best interest was my concern. I knew I would probably be tired at church the next day, but it was worth it to do that for her. We've been married 21 years now and I still want what is best for her! Glory to God!

6. **Never abuse you in any way** – A serious pet peeve of mine is a man that will abuse a woman verbally, physically, or in any way. Remember what 1 Peter 3:7 said? It said…*You husbands in the same way, live with your wives in an understanding way, as*

with someone weaker, since she is a woman; Personally, I just feel that it should be in the nature of a man to want to protect, and care for a woman. There is really something wrong, in my opinion, if a man abuses a woman. I know disagreements can arise and tempers may flare, but a man should NEVER hit a woman. If he is abusive in the dating stage, he is not going to suddenly change after you marry him. DON'T BELIEVE THE LIE THAT HE WILL SUDDENLY CHANGE IF YOU MARRY HIM AND DON'T THINK HIS BEHAVIOR IS YOUR FAULT.

7. **Desire to serve you** – I quoted Ephesians 5:25 earlier which says... *Husbands, love your wives, just as Christ also loved the church and gave Himself up for her.* I read an article by Matthew Ruttan, and in that he was talking about how husbands SHOULD serve their wives. In his article he addresses the verse in Ephesians 5:25. He said that husbands serving their wives is important and then answers why. He said...*Jesus was (and is)* **a servant King.** *He built up the church. He loved the church. He served the church. He taught the church. He pursued the church. He went*

the distance for the church. He prayed for the church. He was patient with the church. He was loyal to the church. He put the church first. He died for the church. That's what a servant King does. And that's supposed to be the same mindset that men have toward their wives! Talk about a game-changer. I wonder why people don't talk about that so much. Hmm. The husband is not supposed to become a slave to the wife and do whatever she says no matter if it is honoring God or not, but he should desire to serve her as Christ served and still serves the church. The happy wife, happy life is not something I think is biblical. I believe both members of the covenant relationship of marriage will make **each other** happy as they are following God's order in their marriage.

Chapter Eight
Final Words

It is my prayer that this book has blessed you in some way. This book is not a call for perfection. We are all a work in progress. However, this book is a call for self examination, and change leading to you being a woman who respects herself and is striving to become the woman God would have her to be. As a result of applying the things learned in this book you will…

1. **Respect God and His will**
2. **Respect yourself**
3. **Get respect from others**

It really all starts with giving your life to Christ and honoring God by your obedience to His will. It is what we all should be doing as Christians. It is very difficult to say you respect yourself when you are living a life of disobedience to God. 1 Corinthians 6:20 says… *For you have been bought with a price: therefore, glorify God in your body.*

You may have made some bad decisions, had some lapses in judgment, failed miserably at a relationship, but now is the time to begin again, and become who God made you to be. Thankfully, God allows second, third, fourth, etc, etc, chances. The word of God says in 1 John 1:9... *If we confess our sins, He is faithful and righteous to forgive us our sins and to cleanse us from all unrighteousness.*

You may have been hurt physically, emotionally, or even spiritually by someone you thought was a man or woman of God. You may have lived with very low self esteem for years, but remember that you have worth, and even though you've experienced trauma, you are still valuable in the eyes of God, and don't allow yourself to be stuck there.

Before you can have a healthy relationship with the man God has for you, make sure you have a healthy self image, and a committed relationship with the first man in your life, and that should be Jesus Christ. If He is setting the standard for your life, you will use wisdom and godly discernment in your relationship choices. You will respect yourself in such a way that you will not feel the need to give yourself away, settle for less than God's best, or compromise in any way. Enjoy your singleness. If and when God sends a man along to find you, the timing will be right. If you are praying to God for Him to send someone your way, remember to make sure you are preparing to be a wife he can truly consider to be his "good thing." If it is God's will for you to have a lifetime of singleness, don't think that something is wrong with you. If that is what God has for you, accept it. However, if it is obvious that a lifetime of singleness is not His will for you, take the wisdom of 1 Corinthians 7:8-9 which says... *But I say to the unmarried and to widows that it is good for them if they remain even as I. But if they do not have self-control, let them marry; for it is better to marry than to burn with passion.*

Take note that it does not say it is better to satisfy your sexual desires with someone, than to burn. It says it is better to **marry** than to burn. Then those desires can be fulfilled.

If you are married and you find yourself struggling in your relationship, pray for God to change things and if you are being abused in any way, seek help from your pastor. Your situation can change. Despite what you may be told by your spouse, you do have great value and potential.

My prayer for you all is that you respect yourself and become the woman God made you to be. You are full of potential. Tap into that potential and blossom. Use the Bible as your primary guide. You will become an asset in the kingdom of God, and a blessing to others.

About the Author

Pastor Calvin M. Hooper has been in ministry for over twenty years and has served as a pastor for more than ten years. He is the founder of the Household of Faith Christian Fellowship Church and the Integrity International Ministerial Fellowship headquartered in Round Rock, TX. His ministry has impacted thousands through the More Like Him Radio Broadcast, currently heard in Texas, Kansas, Missouri, Florida and California, through the Faith Alive Broadcast on iHeart Radio and TuneIn and through his books that have had impact around the world. He has a passion for soul winning, discipleship and community service. Pastor Hooper and his wife, Valerie, have been happily married over 20 years, have five children, and they reside in Round Rock, TX.

www.ingramcontent.com/pod-product-compliance
Lightning Source LLC
LaVergne TN
LVHW051509070426
835507LV00022B/3011

Recognizing & Managing Aggression

Practical Awareness Startegies & Defensive Tactics

Jesse Lawn

Copyright Jesse Lawn 2011

Special Thanks to...

My Wife, Laura, for all of her technical help with the production of this book

Richard Dimitri, for all of the support and friendship over the years

Table of Contents

Introduction	4
Operational Security Model	6
Active Scanning	9
Threat Recognition	12
Personal Perimeter	38
Diffusion and De-escalation	43
Defensive Countermeasures	63
Tactical Disengagement	83
Aid and Evacuation	90
Post-Conflict Police Interaction	101
Conclusion	103
Sources	105

Introduction

What is violence? Violence is generally defined as physical force exerted for the purpose of violating, damaging, or abusing. In reality, violence is a tool. It's not good or bad. It's what we do with it that matters. A police officer who shoots a homicidal maniac on a shooting spree is using violence as a tool for good. A rapist is using violence for evil.

Like it or not, violence is a part of the human experience. Not only is violence used in the commission of crimes, but it determines the boundaries by which we live and is used to enforce the laws of the land. In our society, violence is extremely prevalent…even glorified. Our cinematic heroes are often violent killers. Our video games are graphic simulations of horrific experiences. In general, our social conditioning encourages violence as a means to an end and a way to gain status. Consider the Navy SEALS, for example. Everyone worships those guys. They kill people, lots of people…and they're absolutely our society's heroes.

Before you decide on a personal protection regimen, you first need to make some ethical decisions. Can you use violence? How far are you capable of going to defend yourself? Can you kill another person? Could you gouge out an eye? Some can't. Some religious people are forbidden from such acts, even in self defense. Some physicians and medical professionals refuse to on moral ground. You need to be clear on what you are okay with. For example, if you don't think you can kill someone who's trying to hurt you…don't get a concealed carry license and buy a gun. On the same note, if you don't think you'd have a moral or ethical problem blasting a hole in someone who was trying to kill you…by all means, get a gun. The key here is to evaluate this stuff ahead of time. You don't want to be in a life or death situation, pull out a gun and freeze…only to realize that you can't pull the trigger.

Operational Security Model

Complete personal protection encompasses more than the mere application of physical fighting techniques or the use of a weapon. In order to provide any true measure of safety, we must first step back and look at the bigger picture. Effectively evaluating the grander scheme of things requires specific training and a broader mindset. "Operational security" is a term that refers to the overall ability to perceive and manage threats to your safety. In order to ensure optimum efficiency, it's important to establish and follow a standard model.

Following an appropriate standard model gives you several advantages; it increases your environmental and situational awareness, reduces confusion in the chaos of the moment, demonstrates your commitment to avoiding conflict (which can be quite helpful in court), ensures you act in a just and appropriate manner, and promotes confidence. However, if something is going to be made a standard, it needs to meet certain criteria. An "Operational Security Model" (OSM) must be simple yet practical, versatile, comprehensive, ethical, and legal. The OSM I advocate is comprised of the following components:

- **Active scanning**

- **Threat recognition**

- **Personal perimeter management**

- **Diffusion and de-escalation**

- **Defensive countermeasures**

- **Tactical disengagement**

- **Aid and evacuation**

Here is a brief explanation of the theory behind the OSM; an active scan allows us to perceive potential threats before they are upon us. Once a threat has been identified, we can use a variety of techniques to create space between us and the danger. If the danger is a person, and they aggressively pursue us, often times it's possible to deter them from becoming violent by using verbal skills diffuse the situation. However, because not everyone is reasonable or interested in negotiation, we may need to physically defend ourselves. That's where the defensive countermeasures come in. Using whatever training and tools we have, we fend off a physical assault until it is safe to tactically disengage. Recognize that once the fight is over, the situation may not be completely in hand. If you or someone you are travelling with is wounded…you'll need to render aid and get them and/or yourself to safety.

As you can see, the components all fit together in a supporting cycle. That being said, there are times when steps of the OSM must be skipped or omitted. For example, there is no need to verbally diffuse a situation where someone in a car is trying to run you over. You will want to use all of the other steps…but notice how the OSM is not "hard-and-fast". It's flexible. Further, it facilitates defense of the three primary areas of personal sanctity: physical safety, psychological well being, and personal privacy. These are the three things a bodyguard is required to protect in a client. You are your own bodyguard.

All of my programs and outlines, including this manual, currently follow this OSM.

Active Scanning

Our defensive capabilities are directly related to our awareness. The function of the active scan is to proactively seek out and identify any potential threat. While hostilities and acts of violence certainly constitute serious threats, threats are not necessarily combative in nature. One must remember that environmental hazards such as vehicular traffic, sharp objects, electrical wires, and random obstacles account for more traumatic injuries than violent confrontations. An active scan should provide maximum environmental awareness.

Obviously, the world is a big place, and we cannot possibly scan every inch of our environment as we move about on a daily basis. There's simply too much visual stimuli to process effectively. A good general guideline to follow when conducting an active scan is to survey a 360 degree, 20 ft. "bubble" around you. Based on numerous studies, a 20 ft. "bubble" provides, on average, 1.5 seconds+ to perceive and react to an incoming threat. Seeing what is in front of you at that distance is relatively easy. Keeping a visual on the space behind you takes a little more effort.

To exercise effective 360 degree awareness, keep your head up and look slightly above the horizon in front of you. By looking upwards, your peripheral vision will be able to take a more dominant role in your active scan, enabling you to observe a larger area at one time. Looking up will also help you notice possible threats at or above your head level. Untrained individuals tend to have tunnel vision, looking only at what lies directly in front of them and specific areas of interest. Be sure to survey the entire scene around you by casually looking from side to side. When your head is turned to one side or the other, your peripheral vision will catch people and objects approaching you from the rear. This technique is referred to as the "head-on-a-swivel" by tactical professionals.